# 8 Conversations To Have With Yourself

Contact Johnmartinsr.7@gmail.com for any info on this book.

Other books by Author
www.rodneytheordinarykidchronicles.com
www.8conversationstohave.com

First, I would like to thank everyone in my world that has ever supported me in terms of listening, encouraging, and inspiring me to step into my path. I cannot be anything without great surroundings.

I want to thank my failures as well, as they made me detour, reevaluate, and learn again and again.

I also want to thank my production team for helping me put this product out. Please keep in my corner so we can continue to create great energy. Peace and love to all!

# Table of Contents

# Introduction

First, I am nowhere near being a saint, nor by far the smartest guy on the block. I didn't pay attention in high school, at all. I got expelled from high school and never finished in a traditional setting. I'm not here to tell you I know everything, because the Lord knows I'm not even close. I've made more mistakes than the average, trust me. I know the sun is shining on us all from 93 million miles away, and you feel it just as well as I do. I just want to share my thoughts, that you can think on and reflect. You will be able to grab things from this book to apply to your own life. You will ask yourself great questions to help you move around the world differently. The purpose of this book is to give insight on different perspectives that can help your day to day quests of living your life and feeling good about doing so. Too many of us are just living and not really living happy. Anyway, let's start this book off with a personal mistake I made a few years ago that made me change my whole life. Here you go.

I'm on my way to an early morning flight to New York. I have a meeting at 2pm there, as well as some merchandise to pick up for my mobile business. I pick up my dad on the other side of town to accompany me on this flight. Of course, I am running late but I need to make it work. I'm rushing! I can't miss this flight. I have too many things going for me right now. Plus, every time I pick up merchandise, my business grows so fast. I am chasing money, the story of my life. I pick up my dad and we get to the airport, thanks to me driving 70 mph in a 35 at 5 am. We pull into the airport and I return the rental car I've been driving because of a car accident.

So now picture me and my 69 year-old dad running through the airport. What a sight, right? My heart is damn near jumping out of my chest. Not because I am out of shape, because I was in the most tip of the top and my energy was great. Mainly because I envisioned the gate closing on me and I wouldn't touch the thousands of dollars I was dreaming about the night before. So, off to the races, as I leave my pops in the dust! Of course, he couldn't keep up. I throw my laptop bag on the conveyor belt, and with entitlement, I stare at the TSA lady as to say, "hurry up, I have a flight to catch."

A few minutes go by and people begin to pass me as they go on to their assigned gate. My temper is starting to boil! I take this flight several times a week and they have the audacity to hold me up. Now the police walk up! What is going on? The tall, slender middle-aged European man asks me if the laptop bag he is holding is mine. I turn to him and say with the upmost irritation in my voice, "yes it is! Now can I go? My gate closes in 3 minutes!" The cop just looks at me like he saw a ghost. He says, "I'm afraid you will have to miss that because you have a loaded 9 millimeter with one in the chamber." OMG! I immediately apologize as my heart jumped up into my throat. I couldn't believe the mistake I made. I make this business day trip to New York at least 3 times a week and I would never even think about bringing a loaded gun with me. I felt horrible and stupid and ashamed of myself. How could I make a mistake like this?? I beat myself up bad. I HAD A LOADED GUN IN MY LAPTOP BAG AT THE AIRPORT!! For the sake of my readers, let me explain quickly. I was in a car accident a week prior. I was rear ended pretty hard by a texting driver. Please don't drive and text! Anyway, the dealership finally called me to bring my car in so they could fix it. As I was turning my car over to them, I am grabbing my essentials out from the console. I look down and see my gun that I NEVER take out of my car. I throw it in the laptop bag and that was that. No excuses, I made a mistake. But like my attorney explained to me, people become victims of autopilot. "John, you were moving too fast! You were caught up in the fast money these trips would bring you and you weren't thinking. Routine is how people leave babies in the car." Wow, that was supposed to make me feel better, but it didn't! How did I let myself get off my square and be so careless?

Needless to say, I got through that situation with a minor misdemeanor. It could have been a lot worse. What if I would have gotten to NY with that bag? They have very strict gun laws. I would still be locked up.

Two things I've heard since I was a child is, 1) God works in mysterious ways, and 2) Timing is everything. This whole incident couldn't have happened at a worse time. I felt I was in control when really, my relationship with my girlfriend at the time was failing. I was moving backwards chasing money like I was in the early 2000's. I was experiencing PTSD flare ups from a tragic event that took place at one of my night life events, and so much more. But this experience changed me in two ways. One, it gave me a chance to sit and think about myself! The more I did this, the more I realized I didn't know myself as well as I thought. And the 2nd thing it did for me was gave me the opportunity to sit and think about what is truly important. It gave me the chance to evaluate my moves and how I can be my own worst enemy. I learned that I am never happy. I learned that I stay busy to cover pain. I also learned that whatever the situation is, it could be worse.

I'm also thankful for that event in my life. It woke up the questions within me, ABOUT me. I needed to have some real conversations with myself about my life. I needed to confront the compulsive side of me that chases money. I needed to understand that I don't have to be perfect and even if I tried to be, I would fail miserably.

Going through life and not really knowing ourselves is quite common. We know ourselves as the employee. You know, the one that gets up early to go punch a clock. We know our skills on that specific job. We know exactly how much "ignorance" we are going to tolerate from our co-workers LOL. We know ourselves as a parent. You know what you will do if your kids get out of line. You know what you will tolerate from them. We know ourselves as a friend. We can talk about countless times we have been there for someone. One thing that airport situation made me realize is that I don't know my weaknesses as well as I thought. I didn't know my "triggers" of impulse. I spent years running and taking care of everyone else, I didn't know what makes me tick, and what makes my tock.

Some people don't get acquainted with themselves until they have raised their kids and are of retirement age. At this point, they want to do everything they ever dreamed. But let's take the approach of learning ourselves while we are young. I believe learning ourselves while we are in the best shape of our lives opens our world up to opportunities we can actually take advantage of. It sharpens our wit and strengthens our core. We become the best version of us, which enhances life around us. The younger you are when you become self-aware, the healthier and more rewarding your life will be growing into your older years. Don't just work, work, work! Find a healthy balance of taking "me" time and enjoy your world. Learn yourself!

I share my airport mistake because for one, it's real. I don't want to ever represent fake. And also, I learned tremendous value from that mistake. I watch myself now. I check myself when I start to see my "inner bag chaser" coming out. I'm self-aware of who I am and how detrimental I am to myself if I don't grow. I learn myself and understand I can learn from a baby. I open this book with peace and love and hope going forward in these next chapters you find value, and at least something to hold on to.

## First Conversation

# What breaks my momentum?

We have all been there. A great idea comes to our heads and we get excited. We are full of life and energy pertaining to this idea, we can't wait to get started. We can't wait to tell someone, either. this is when it gets tricky! Now telling someone so early might be a mistake. We might tell the wrong person. We don't even have the whole idea or concept completely thought out, but we feel we need to tell someone IMMEDIATELY. So, we rush to the nearest phone to call our co-worker, business partner, spouse, brother, sister, or dog. With all the enthusiasm and energy in us, we pour our heart and ideas out all over this person, only to hear a dull and/or negative response. Now there is a difference between constructive and positive positions, and just downright negative and pessimistic positions. All you hear from this individual is negativity and it immediately kills your vibe. You start second guessing your own thought that was so overwhelmingly a "for sure win." Next thing you know your dream is silenced and overshadowed by this individual's "that won't work" attitude. It happens all the time for me and others. I can bet this has happened to you as well. This is called a shift in momentum. The euphoric feeling your own thoughts brought to you was bamboozled and shot down by someone that just simply didn't "catch the wave". They didn't see all the positives and THAT is perfectly ok. It's not their dream, their vision, their idea. What is NOT ok is you giving your power away! What do I mean by this? It is simple. God gifts you with several ideas and visions and paints pictures that become clear as day- IF, you put the right energy towards them. Once you transfer the energy to someone (by telling them your idea) that isn't very receptive, you must recognize that THIS is ok and take your energy back! Don't allow someone to "kill your vibe" or drown out your vision. Take it back and keep the momentum on high. I know, it is tough. Especially when you tell someone that you value your great idea and they "shit" on it. But hey, you need to realize early that people don't see the same way. Just because there might be a mutual love between the two of you, doesn't mean they will automatically feel what you are explaining. It's human nature, get over it. That is why there are several hundreds of brands of the same products. Go to your local grocery store and walk down the potato chip isle and you will see several different brands of chips to appeal to several different audiences. There is something for everyone, and your ideas are no different. 7 billion people in the world and all you need are a couple hundred thousand lol. Keep your power. Control your momentum. Tell yourself to keep moving forward.

There are several other ways you can kill your momentum. The core of these reasons come from your own toxic and negative thoughts. If you are trying to motivate yourself, stay in a positive light because the moment you tell yourself anything that is negative, you take a chunk out of your momentum. You will start to move slower, think of distractions, listen more to others, drown your own positive voice out. You might be having a bad moment and let it destroy your whole day and now you are wishing you had at least 12 of those hours back. It happens. Over and over. We are human. The key is to recognize these behaviors and nip them in the bud early so you can stay above the water and maintain a mindset of excellence. Even in a life crisis, your mindset will make or break you. You can not have a bad day, only bad moments.

Life crisis. Death, relationship break ups, friendship feuds, automobile breaking down, fired from jobs, kids causing stress, etc. All are difficult to deal with. You might have had a great day in your car detail business. You cleaned 10 cars at 200 dollars a pop. At the end of the day, you are smiling on your way to your car to go home and your car won't start. You live on the other side of town and now you need to figure out how you are going to make it to work in the morning. Handle it! This is a part of life. You might have to take everything you just made and put it into your car, but don't lose your momentum. Don't use this car "crisis" to cancel the three appointments you have in the morning. Those three appointments help you keep your momentum high. Any slack up will cause you to lack sooner than later.

Keeping your momentum high is tough work. It takes tremendous focus and discipline. You can do it though. It will require you to do a few things.

One, it will require you to evaluate your circle of friends and family. You must evaluate the people around you and put them in categories. Nothing is wrong with doing this. You love all your people, but you can't "invite everyone to the party." You can't tell your cousin John about a great business idea you have and expect great insight from him if he has never experienced business. Well, you can tell him, but understand who you are talking to when you get a response. Know how to take good info and leave the bad. You aren't "too good" to receive information from anyone. You can learn from a baby. But you need to understand the source and this requires evaluating them. This way you don't give your power away by crying and giving up on your passion because your cousin John told you your idea sucks. But John doesn't like to take risks at all and is very content with same routine every day. Maybe you need to think out your vision to the point you keep the energy high. It is your gift.

You may not need a partner, you may need a worker. Once you develop your whole vision then you can delegate. Get my drift?

Another way you can keep your momentum high is by setting small goals that are attainable for your task. Be as realistic as you can. Don't start a cookie bakery service and expect 3,000 orders your first week if you don't have any marketing and advertising. If your enthusiasm drives you to set high goals, make sure you are meeting all areas in order to maintain this because if you don't, you will kill some of your momentum once you don't hit that big goal. You will disappoint yourself and now you are not putting the same energy into your business. But if you say to yourself, "once I hit 500 orders, I will celebrate and then set my next goal of 500 more", you are keeping a positive mindset that will keep growing.

Reflection: Am I the killer of my own dreams? Sure, I am if I let other people talk me out of my own thoughts. Why do I allow someone to have that much power over me? I need to change this and start living my life for purpose and my wants and needs. This way I can add more to my surroundings. Not everyone is capable of creating ideas. This is something I may be taking for granted. Thoughts pop into my head all the time but do I utilize them? A lot of the time I think of the work that is required and I give up before I start. I don't put enough effort and energy into figuring out easier ways to create and bring my thoughts to life. Let's change this today. Let's be more mindful and intentional of recognizing when I'm being my own "buzz killer". Human beings are creators. We are the only species on Earth that can create what we do. Don't block yourself from creating.

Call to Action: This is my goal for the week. I should carry a notebook around or open my notes on my phone. I should write out the closest 10 people that are in my circle. (Most people will have less than 10). Think about conversations over the years. Figure out who can help with ideas or who I need to call when it's all mapped out so I can delegate some task. Figure out who are Debby Downers, so I don't make the mistake of sharing too much, IF I can't control the transfer of energy. The energy that is given to me is up to me to keep and hold high. I am accountable for my actions and my thoughts. I need to realize my gifts are unique to me and not everyone is supposed to roll with what is mine. That is ok. Keep moving, even if it is small steps. It is better than "dropping out of the race."

I need you to understand that bouncing ideas off of people is great! We need to do this. It creates great energy when you know who you are sharing with! Also, when you can discern constructive feedback and just negative feedback. Don't let either hold you back. Let's go!

## Second Conversation

# Be ok with change. Adapt! Ask yourself, is routine keeping me from being happy.

Just like this book has several chapters, so does life. Every chapter is different and has different tasks, people and feelings. Some of us struggle with wanting to bring everyone we met in the previous chapter, to the next chapter and our lives don't work like this. Life-long friends are rare. When we are younger, a lot of us adopt an attitude of thinking change is bad. I've heard several of my friends say things like, "I'm never going to change," with a look of accomplishment and wanting kudos, or points for not changing behaviors. We must realize changing is growing. Change is good. Change is what's needed in a world that changes every day. If you haven't noticed our world moves at a super-fast pace. The internet has made the opportunity for this to be totally different tomorrow. If you work for a big corporation, I bet you feel a change or two, very often. Many CEO's of large companies read 50 or more books a year. Why? Because they constantly need to gain different perspectives. They need to keep moving, but at a speed to understanding constant change. If CEO'S change their minds and approaches daily for business to be successful, why do we as humans feel we don't need to change our ways for our lives to be successful? The "never change" mindset is pure stagnation. Let's take social media for example. Look over your Facebook and go back a few years and read some of your previous posts. Do some of your posts sound ridiculous? The world has changed, so the views you had a few years ago might be different today. The world requires change, and the people that have a mindset to stay the same get left behind.

Some of our structures and moral principles even change over time. We might have believed God wasn't real at one point and our life experiences have led us to believe otherwise, or vice versa. It is totally your call.

Look at your lives and think back at some of the things you would like a do over on. I bet some of the reasons are because you would have handled them differently with your newer ways of thinking.

When I'm on the East coast, especially in New York, I talk faster. They just talk fast and if I want to get a point across, I need to blend into my environment. Midwest, not so much. We talk slower.

Some of us adults hate trying new things. We also are very stuck in one way of thinking. It takes 17 times of repetition to develop a habit. A habit is only an action we are "comfortable" doing. That is all it is. Doesn't mean it's a good thing or a bad thing. It is simply something we have grown to do and be comfortable doing it. If this is the case, most of us have a great deal of comfort. We are very routine. We like our "things" a certain way. We don't even want to explore a different option. We don't want to learn new tricks. Let me say this.

Not being willing to learn and change CRIPPLES relationships, and our growth, and of course knowledge. Relationships? Sure. In order to develop a great relationship with our kids, we must learn to speak another language. Yes, we must learn how to talk with them so they can understand. We might have to listen to their music to see what is going on in their world and the influences that are helping to change them.

I had the privilege of helping my daughter with her 8th grade math homework. I say privilege with every sarcastic bone in my body. Anyway, her homework looked foreign. The way they are learning algebra is totally different from when I learned. I panicked. I felt dumb. I felt like I couldn't help her. So, what do I do? I resort to my old ways and show her how I learned. Well, some things that might work, but with this situation it caused frustrations. She said to me, "dad, I have to do it the way the teacher is teaching else I will get in trouble. They want to see the problem written out like this," as she points at the instructions. So of course, I throw my hands up and tell her, "I don't know." I shouldn't have. I should have opened my brain and tried to learn a new way of doing this so I could help my daughter. This example is common, not just with schoolwork. We usually like to teach our ways of doing things with our kids. That is great, but we must understand change and communication barriers. We might sound foreign to them. It is not ok, just because we are comfortable in our ways, to just disregard other ways. Let's not cripple ourselves. When you learn something new, how do you feel? Me, I feel great! I love learning new hobbies. I go to the shooting range quite frequently nowadays. I used to just like handguns and for years, I would tell myself that I'm just a handgun shooter. I told myself I don't like big guns. Well, boy did I miss out on some fun for many years. Now, I have added AR's, Techs and shotguns to my shooting range joy. I can honestly say I have a greater time and a more appreciation for my new way of doing this hobby of mine. I really look forward to my hobby as more than just therapy now. It's exciting! This is just a small example of how trying new things add so much more to your life. Changing up your routine adds fun, a sense of freshness can rejuvenate you. You owe yourself a great time on Earth. It's up to you to keep your flame burning and really get the most out of your moments. Change as much as you need. We are here for a short moment. Our lives should have some excitement.

Reflection: There are some things I would like for us to take away from this chapter.

One, learn how to invite the thought of change, our perception of change needs to be in a positive light, so we encourage it. This will require you to unlearn some things and relearn some new ways. You might have to learn how to learn. What works for me might not work for you, so find out the easy ways to learn and learn all you can. It will help your surroundings and keep your brain full of growth and youth. Secondly, realize when you are being an "old head." Stop and think in the middle of some activities. You will recognize how stagnate you are being. Liven your walk through your life. Some of us just need a refreshing new outlook. Last, but not least realize if you need to change your playmates and playgrounds. You must study you and your surroundings. Your playground might be holding you back. Your playmates might be holding you back. Well you are allowing it. Am I stuck?

Call to action: Be intentional for the next few weeks to take some "me time". It doesn't need to be a long period of time. It could be 20 minutes a day to try something new. Just YOU, not your playmates. Change up the playground and see a different perspective. Read! Read books, read yourself, read your feelings, read your interpretations. Read your views. And change when you can. Open up YouTube and watch a "how to" video of something you've always wanted to try and DO IT! Hey, if you find yourself not liking it, oh well. That was the worst that can happen. But what if you try it and you LOVE it? You might have changed your whole life for the better. Your next chapter might just be the best chapter of your life!

## Third Conversation

# Are you living in YOUR moments?

Can I tell you something? Most of us are not present. We have been given a gift, which is NOW and we don't even appreciate it. You don't believe me? Let's break down your day. Of course, I might not hit your scenario completely, but follow along and tweak your schedule accordingly.

Your alarm goes off because you need to get up and get ready for work. You try to stay in bed a little longer, to get your mind together because you aren't "up" all the way. You hit that snooze button, but you regretfully leave the cozy of your bed to go brush your teeth and wash up. You throw your clothes on and out the door you go to be in the midst of everyone else "living the life" of work. How many times after you got up out of bed did you think about your past? Or your future? Present? The latter, I bet not as much. You arrive to work and you immediately start working. You are living in the moment now, huh? Of course, you are because you are responding to emails, tasks, and orders. You are getting to it! Well good for you, but this isn't your time. These aren't your moments.

It's finally lunch time. You have a group that you go to lunch with usually and talk about family and vacations and everything else, which is fun, but today you have some errands to run and some bills to pay. While you are paying your bills and calling to set up a dentist appointment for your child, you stuff a fast food sandwich down your throat. You have 3 minutes before you need to be back to work, so you run to the bathroom and release. As you release, you text someone important in your life because they are on your mind. You finish your workday and go home to do some cooking, cleaning or whatever else you need to do in order to keep going. Then it's 9pm and you finally can sit down and relax. You fall asleep in 5 minutes. And the routine is the same the next day. What are you doing for YOU? If we had to name who owns each moment in our day, you would own the least. Your employer, your kids, your spouse, your enemy, your friends, and everything else consumes your thoughts and your time. 50, 000 things cross your mind a day and you taking a deep breath and realizing where your world is, is rarely one of them. We are either thinking about the future and what we need to do later or, we are thinking of the past. We all know how thinking of our past can be detrimental to our health, for some. We need to still freeze moments of our lives and be in tune with how we are thinking at the moment. Not auto-pilot. But just being in tune. You remember the gun situation at the airport, right? That was me not being in the moment. That was thinking 5 steps ahead and not checking the present step. We must value the moment we are in. You will smile more. You will feel your heartbeat. You will look at yourself in the mirror and see the glow others see. Or you will see the gloom that you can change. Either way, you can be in control of right now right this second! It is crucial we grab our present moments. We sometimes dwell on the past and when we do this, we are subliminally taking away from right NOW. How can we match energy around us if we are only producing at 70%? The other 30% is dwelling on some mistakes you made in the past. We must get over these mistakes. How? Great question! First, we must forgive our past. We must think of the past as a steppingstone to where we are at right this second. We couldn't be here right this second, if our past didn't help us evolve to this present state. Ask yourself, "what if everything that has happened in my life was for me to know all I know right this second?" "What if my higher power intentionally pushed me along the path I traveled, so I can have the knowledge and experience to do what I am doing RIGHT NOW?" " What am I doing? Is my purpose to expand from my past? My present is important. I need to live right now.

Reflection: Your present is your gift. The weather is your gift. Enjoy them. I know we all must work and give up a lot of our time to the daily grind. But within these days, value the moment. Have a quick reset. Step out of the board meeting and have a 45 second walk. In that walk, think about your life right now. Where are you? Think about how you feel. Think about what you have. The greatest way you can show your appreciation to anything, is by giving your time and paying attention to it.

Pay attention to your moments. Be in tune with your moves. Appreciate what you have right now. What do I have right now? The greatest gift of all, and that is time.

Call to Action: Stop right now and take a break. Close your eyes and breathe in DEEP. Exhale slowly. Feel your heartbeat. Ask yourself "who am I?" I bet you will be shocked at what you say. It sounds weird but take a second to get to know you as much as you know your job at work. Each time you think about a memory, counter it with a present thought. This takes training your mind, but as we know conditioning is needed for us to take control. Balance is key. If you think about your future, come right back with a present thought about you and how you feel. "What am I thinking? Are they positive thoughts? Are they unhealthy thoughts? Hmmm. The choice is yours to live in the NOW.

## Fourth Conversation

# Your chip on your shoulder is noticeable

One thing I love is a good party! I love seeing people enjoy themselves. I was in the nightclub business for quite some time, and I enjoyed MOST of that time. It was the times that the wrong energy would be present, it would make it unbearable for me. I would sometimes leave my own party and go stand outside and get some fresh air. I remember times surveying the line of people at the door waiting to get in. Occasionally, I would have to "check someone's temperature". This is when I see someone in line looking mad at the world, and I go talk to them. "What's up bruh. How are you feeling tonight? It's going to be a great night, plenty of ladies in there, man." Or, "you good bro? You at a night club man, smile. You supposed to be having fun." Or " Damn baby girl, I know you didn't get all pretty and your hair done to look so mad. What's wrong? What are you drinking?"

I understand there are several reasons people come out to a night club. Some are stressed from a week of work and want to unwind. Some want to have a good time. Some want to start trouble with the world because they aren't happy. Whatever the reason is, it was my duty to understand my patrons. A lot of people aren't self-aware of the energy and aura they are putting off into the world. Just because you don't see yourself and your bad vibes, doesn't mean no one else does. Matter of fact, people are very good at picking up signals from others. So, if I am throwing a party and I let a person in that is displaying a bad aura, that will change the mood of the surroundings. You need to be careful.

Me and my security staff became so good at diffusing situations, because we started to identify the "regulars" that would come in with the attitudes. Often, it's the same few people that always seem to have a dark cloud over them. They are upset with something, or someone. Are you that person? Do you have a chip on your shoulder that you haven't dealt with? A lot of us are going through life right now with a lot of baggage. We haven't dealt with certain situations from our past that affect us every day. Or maybe we aren't appreciating the moments we have been gifted right NOW, so we are walking around acting as if someone owes us. No one owes us anything. Not one single person on this planet owes you anything. I know it sounds unfair, but whatever you do for someone does not have to be reciprocated. It just doesn't! In a fair world, good deeds should be exchanged, but we know that isn't the case.

93 % of communication is nonverbal. Body language says it all. When you are talking to someone, the first thing we notice is your tone of voice, but that isn't the most important thing we notice. We notice your looks. We notice how you stand, how your body projects your sounds. You can literally say whatever you want us to believe, but without your body language speaking, your audience will be confused. Oftentimes, we aren't controlling our look. Our negative thoughts consume us and they start to bleed out from within. People can see it. Don't reject the help someone is offering you. The truth of the matter is, they may not understand how to help you, but

they are reaching out because they see the hurt. They see the picture you are painting for the world and they want to add some vibrant colors to it.

Reflection: Out of the several things you need to know in life, one is do not insult the next man's intelligence. Pay attention to feedback that you receive from peers. If people tend to make it a point to move away from you, there is a reason. People shouldn't feel anxiety when you come around. You should never inflict ill thoughts in someone. Your thoughts you have come out. The way you think is exhibited in the way you move. Work on you, so you can scrape that chip off of your shoulder and stretch out and enjoy life ♡□

Call to Action: Work! Work on you! As you can tell, the narrative of this book clearly states to study YOU! Work on your insecurities. Work on identifying triggers. Eliminate the word "hate" from your vocabulary. Talk life into yourself. Speak encouraging words, even if you haven't got to the point to believe them yet. You will! Repetition, habit, reinforcement, keep moving.

There is a thin line between love and hate. They are both feelings and emotion. Flip them. Learn to love what you hate. How? Find something good in something you hate and focus on that. In elementary, I used to have a bully that I hated! He would pick on me to the point I would cry. Now we are friends and I can look back and honestly love the fact that he was persistent in trying to get what he wanted. I know that may sound weird, but flip things to benefit you! Me looking at him as a persistent, determined young boy made me come to an understanding that actually benefit me. It took the "hate" away and now I have no bad energy that negatively affects me. Try it, it's hard but worth it. This method won't work for everything. Some things are too hurtful to just forgive without serious professional counseling. But the majority of stuff we just nonchalantly hate, can be reversed. We get into the habit of hating things, not realizing the power of hate consumes our whole existence. It drains our energy and really takes a toll on our bodies. That chip on your shoulder isn't deserving of your life. It's weighing you down.

## Fifth Conversation

# You have a gift, but do you know what it is?

So, out of 168 hours a week, the average adult should sleep about 50 of those hours away. We also work 40 hours and spend an additional 10-15 hours a week preparing for those 40 work hours. Think about the rest of the time you have. How many hours are devoted to your family? If you are like the rest of us, you have about 20 hours a week devoted to yourself. 20 a week? What does that tell me? That tells me we are caught up in a fast-paced race and we haven't taken the time to learn ourselves. We don't know ourselves. We know our job task better than anyone. We know our spouse's mood swings better than they do. We know how many times our kids will ask us for something the first 10 minutes we step foot in a room. BUT, do you know what you like? I bet peace and quiet, huh? We can't wait to tap in to the 50 hours a week that we use for sleep. But what about our gifts? We each have a gift to give the world and make us feel whole. I'm not saying we aren't whole, because we are. But FEELING whole is not always so common. We each have a purpose. Are you going to wait until after you retire at 65 to figure out what that gift is? I get it, we have priorities. We need to set ourselves up for a promising future, so our focus is working vigorously and sleeping when we can. But what about our purpose?

I feel my purpose is to be a writer and share my easy to follow approach and my perspectives with the world. If I didn't take time out for myself and take my time back for me, I would have never sold over 1,000 books my first year of writing. May not be a lot to you, but me finding this out at 39 was a huge step for me. If I was still sitting at that job for 40 hours a week and then running around for everyone else when I got off, I would have never discovered this talent. I wouldn't have had the time to devote to hours of writing. I have always been a writer. Ever since I was young, I would write whole football games through commentating. I was always writing. But just now recently focused on this because I created the time to do so.

I learn so much from others. I intentionally seek knowledge from others. I look for something that will inspire me, attract me, or simply show me a different way. I can honestly say I learn from everyone. I say that to say this. I allow myself to see the gift in others. I give myself the time to view it. A lot of the time, the gift I see is not seen by that particular person. When I point out something I appreciate in someone, I often get a surprised response like, "hmm I don't know. I never thought about that." Or, "really? You think I would be great at doing that?"

Let's not wait until we are 70 to discover ourselves and our talents. Yes, we have kids to raise. Yes, we must make money every single day. Yes, we have life stresses that need dealt with early. Yes, yes, yes! But learn you. Take time to get in tune and learn as you handle all of your life's dealings. You have a gift inside of you that you must unleash for us, your surroundings and more importantly you and your growth!

Reflection: Be solid to you. Wake up wanting to be more in tune with you. Your family, your job, your bills, your world must get the best version of you. You give us the best version of you by learning who you are. You can't create the best running shoe if you don't study what it takes to make the best running shoe. But research will allow you to bring the best ingredients to life.

Call to Action: Have you noticed a routine with all of these "action plans"? They are pleading for you to create TIME for yourself. Put yourself first. Think back to you as a child. What talents did people say you had? Some of us were so shy, we didn't allow others to see our talents. But what did you like? Build off of this. Try doing something you liked back then and see how much you have evolved with that skill. Because this takes you right into chapter 6.

## Sixth Conversation

# Our route has detours

I remember sitting Indian style on the floor in kindergarten with everyone else. Mrs. Williams asked what we wanted to be when we grew up. We each went around the room and we all said things like doctors, lawyers, police officers, etc. I know very few people from back then, however the ones I know didn't choose to be what they said in kindergarten. I know I didn't. Life happens. We get stuck in everyday dramas and pitfalls sometimes.

But here is what I remember from that kindergarten memory. Everyone was so excited! I even had my hand up hella high and couldn't wait to tell my teacher I wanted to be a boxer. Everyone was inching towards her with pure enthusiasm about our futures. You couldn't cut the energy in the room with a knife, you would have needed something much bigger! So, what happened? Because the little kid in us had it all figured out. Our kindergarten version had so much positive energy, huh? What happened? Again, I ask that because over time, we learn more. Over time we grow more. Over time, we are equipped to become the best us. So, what happened to the energy? We aren't as enthused as we were in our younger years? Which science tells us maybe we should be more enthused. I'm not knocking anyone's hustle when I say this, I love to work, regardless if it's for myself or someone else, but in kindergarten when you were asked what you wanted to be when you grew up, no one said I want to be an analyst for Wells Fargo(which is a great career). But did you settle? Or, was the life struggles too much to get back on your route? Did you get distracted? Now again, nothing is wrong with working for Wells Fargo, or having any other job for that matter. But what made us say, to hell with what we actually want to do and let me fill out this app and hope I'm "good" enough they call me to come do what they tell me to do. You had a dream of being an artist, a songwriter and everything else under the sun. Now don't just work and pay bills. Here goes that TIME word again. Your time should be directed towards what gives you energy. Give your time value and fight for what you want. If you want to be a songwriter, write songs on your lunch break! Devote time to your "other hustle". I'm not saying throw that analyst job away! I'm saying ADD to your hustle because you need that school kid energy to breathe life into you. Your job maybe very rewarding, but it's not your dream. If it is, dream more because your dreams carry you to new heights.

I get it, our routes get switched daily by life's challenges and we need to change lanes, directions and ideas ALL the time. But what we do too often is just change and forget what we want. Me personally, I was miserable working a 9 to 5 and raising kids. I knew I needed to do more, but by the time I had bills and everything else to deal with, I was tired and didn't devote any time to my crafts or goals. I was in a routine of waking up before my body was ready, going to work and working all day at a job I didn't enjoy, just to come home and give my family a little piece of me before exhaustion set in and I would repeat this daily. I kept asking myself, "is there more to life." I would ignore the burning desire to create things. I would block out images of me during my dreams of "making it big" doing what I wanted. It was hard for me to be happy knowing I was living everyday adding stress to my life because I wasn't doing what I wanted to do. I'll give you a real-life example of how detours set us on a different route. I started a company several years ago that focused on the development of my community. I spread social awareness of issues that plagued the community by "partying with a purpose". I would produce family friendly fun events and take proceeds of events and donate them to several organizations to spark change. The company grew so big that we started producing night life entertainment. One year, during one of our annual events, the event was going just as planned and it was very exciting to see hundreds of people gathered at this party. Everyone was dancing and having a good time and during this event, we started to plan the next year's annual party. We were going to double the budget and bring some headline entertainment. That's how you must work! Plan your next steps while the momentum is high. We already locked the venue and the date down for the following year. Well, the last two minutes of the party was life changing. after most of the people left for the evening, two people were killed in the parking lot. Totally unexpected. The incident stemmed from some outside drama that had nothing to do with my party. Well, things changed in the blink of an eye. I felt my whole future just collapsed. I had big plans of the event getting much bigger every year, but I immediately said to hell with that. After a couple of weeks of depression and analyzing, I decided to change the direction of my company. I was about to end it all and then I thought about my purpose. I changed my company into a marketing company that would still be beneficial to the needs of small businesses in my area. We have been in business ever since and we have created some great plays for businesses all over this country. I feel that my purpose is still being fulfilled, I just had to change my route. It happens to us all. We can't lose sight of the prize. Bad things may happen. Your life may seem like it's over. Trust me, you aren't the only one that goes through those moments. But instead of asking yourself, "why me?" Ask yourself, "why NOT me?" You can handle it! Adversity is your middle name. You are great at changing your route. Now perfect your detours to set up the best advantage for YOU, not just your surroundings. We are going to have challenges from whatever we decide to do. Detours and roadblocks are a part of every situation. The sooner we learn how to adapt and maneuver through these obstacles it is better for us. It equips us, and our fight gets easier, or maybe harder, but that's life, right? Fight through it! We get one world to roam through.

Reflection: After reading this chapter, what did you think about? Did you think about that kid you were in kindergarten? You still have that energy, but it's suppressed. The foods and thoughts you have let into your body control that energy. Start thinking power. Power thoughts! What is it that you want?

Call to Action: Right now, I need you to come up with a contingency plan. Your plan should be a small goal for this week, but your plan should be at least 3 plays deep. Each play is a detour to your goal. We need to see a plan A, B, and C. As you start to do these plans more often, you will begin to develop more and more plans. You deserve this great skill set. It will boost your views to a whole new level. The game is chess, not checkers.

## Seventh Conversation

# What are you waiting on?

Let me start by asking you a real question. For every action, when does it start? It's a real question lol. The action starts by the thought. For example, you want to start a fitness center, right? The start of your journey started with that thought of, 'hey, I want to open a fitness center'. What is next? HAHA! That's where we get tripped up and lose our momentum. Why? I believe some of us, including me think that every time we have a great idea, someone is supposed to drop from the sky to our aid and we tell them what to do and then, BAM, there's our fitness center. I also believe that you and I think about our idea and realize, it's not perfect timing and we wait! Let's just get one thing clear for the rest of our lives. There is no such thing as "perfect timing"!!! Never utter those words ever again. Our thoughts come to us as gifts. It is our job to create them. Now, sometimes I get a few thoughts that I just end up not wanting to do after thought and consideration. However, there are some really good ideas I WANT to do, but the "timing" is "off". So, it is our jobs to figure out how to make our plans work, when we get these ideas, regardless of the situation. You can respond to everyone asking you "what happened" by saying, "man, I just have too much going on." Sometimes we can feel that way, but it's not what we do, it's how we do it. And progression needs to happen daily. It doesn't have to be a large leap to show progress. Progress might just be standing up getting ready to take a step. So, for the example of the fitness center, progress might be to make a phone call to find out what the price of 12 treadmills will be. This helps you get one step closer.

We must realize until the day we are resting forever, we will always have "a lot going on". We will always encounter moments that demand our attention more than our dreams. We will always have "a lot going on," so timing is never just going to be perfect. What does perfect timing look like? I always think "perfect timing" sounds like easy with no work. Like, "I can't open up my coffee shop right now because the place needs a makeover. It's just not the right time." Of course, it's the right time. Get to work giving the place a makeover and again, get to work. Put that work in and create your perfect timing.

I remember I had a comedy show scheduled, and 48 hours prior, I had my wisdom teeth pulled. Now every promoter knows that right before your event, people will start blowing your phone up for tickets. Seems like every show, last minute sales go through the roof. So, 48 hours before the show, I'm getting my wisdom teeth pulled. But guess what? I didn't stop my route and my hustle. I stuck that gauze in my mouth and started getting to the sales. I drove myself around and touched a lot of people that would not have come if I couldn't get them tickets. Mouth numb and all, I had to make the situation work. If not, the seats would have been empty and the comedians wouldn't have had good energy. I love the energy rapper 50 Cent brought to the rap game in the late 90's. My understanding of 50 Cent's early years was that he was having trouble getting attention from the rap world. He was putting some energy out, but it just wasn't grabbing attention. He didn't sell any music and record labels weren't checking for him. For the average person, this could have been when a lot of us said, "the timing isn't right, let me go back to my comfort zone and try again later." For most of us that later turns into never. But what 50 Cent did next shocked the world. He knew he had to create momentum. He understood that there is no time like the present. He started moving at an incredible pace and he put out the song "How To Rob," which was talking about robbing all of the major rappers in the game at that time. That song took New York by storm and had a lot of rappers heated about it. He created energy and CREATED his TIME! Needless to say, he went on to becoming one of the most remembered rappers and successful businessmen of our time. Just think if he would have never kept going. Just think if he would have never kept thinking of a way. Just think if he didn't CREATE TIME! Trust me, the world doesn't know whatever idea you have to bring into this world. How can you allow the world to tell you it's not time for it? You must tell yourself it is time and create your energy! "Make room, world, here I come!"

Reflection: Boss up! We aren't promised tomorrow. We can't think about tomorrow as if it is around the corner. We must think about the present and how we can make impact today! Remember playing with Legos when you were younger? You would sit there and start building things one piece at a time. Well, treat your life that way. Once you start to take control of your moments, momentum builds. Get to moving and watch your time create the moment. When you put energy into something, the universe grabs it. The universe aids and assists your path. It's up to you to keep putting one foot in front of the other. Start living in the moment and claim your time!

Call to Action: We must figure out what we want to consume our time with. What is it that you want to manifest? When you figure out what and who you want to be, step into that title. Step into the light and move like you don't have another day to make it happen. I like to call each move a play. Make plays all day long to make sure you are triumphant. The more you do, the less you will need to do later. Focus on your focus and start living now, because it's your time.

## Eighth Conversation

# Life happens to all of us, keep moving!

What makes your story so much more devastating than the next person's story? Why do you feel like you're the only one that goes through things? Probably because you feel your pain, and this is fine. But the next person is probably thinking, "man, I grew up poor too", or "I watched my parents go through an abusive relationship too," "I lost my job too," or "I am fighting my addiction too", "I lost my best friend too". Never want to make life seem easy, but we are all going through life. Life entails trauma, love, heartache and pains and everything else for EVERYONE! We must learn how to deal. We also must learn to respect the fact that "it's not just me". How are some coping and getting through despite all of their hardships, and some people are "failing" at life? Mindsets. What you tell yourself matters. How many times you fall doesn't matter to someone that is determined to make it to the finish line. The person that is determined is going to just get right back up, brush their knees off and get to moving again. While they are down on the ground after they fell, what are they telling themselves? Some of us would say things like, "I can't do this anymore," "I hurt so bad", "someone help me." some of us would say, "get up! Let's go, we can't quit!" "I'm better than this!" "Man, let's fight!" "I fell again? Watch me get back up and keep moving!" Situations we incur can make us or break us. What is our perspective as we partake in these life's situations. I will always admire my grandpa. He was a great man that never raised his voice. He always had a joke to tell the world. Regardless of what was going on, you can see him thinking and trying to figure out the positives in the situation. Without him knowing, I would watch him. I would watch how he moved and how he would speak. He would always pause before he spoke. He would think out his thoughts clearly. He had a wit to him that was unique. The kind of wit that after hearing a few words he spoke, you knew he could say a lot more, but chooses not to. Maybe he did know I was watching him. Maybe he moved calculated because he was trying to set the best example he could for his grandchildren. Maybe he just trained himself to be so poised over the years. Maybe he was dealing with pain? He was a quiet man. He didn't say much unless you started the conversation. Who knows, and the world will never know because he isn't with us. However, I did take away this valuable lesson from him. Keep moving! Even when he was still, you could tell he was thinking. Regardless of what life hit him with, he smiled. Regardless of how bad the situation was, he seemed like he had it together.

I use my grandpa as an example because he was a fighter. But he fought in ways that you really didn't see, you just saw the end result. You saw a man that was smart, he knew when to speak. You saw a man that always seemed to be calm, he was very disciplined. You saw a guy that would try and make you laugh with his dry humor. Sometimes it worked, sometimes it didn't, but he wouldn't stop. These are all results from a man that went through hardships. But the results come from tremendous self-discipline and self-love. He controlled his emotions. He moved on his own principles and values. I believe the more we are in tune with ourselves and what we believe in, the better we can deal with life. Everyone needs a foundation. Foundations start and maintain our structure. We need to learn ourselves. Knowledge of self is our foundation. It makes it so we can deal with anything that is thrown our way. You might wake up tomorrow and walk into your job and they have your box on your desk. They don't need you anymore. What are you going to do? You need to keep living. You might wake up and the world is going through a pandemic. What are you going to do? Your best friend might have died in a car accident last night and you open Facebook and see the news. What are you going to do? You might buy a car and right when the warranty expires, your transmission needs replaced. Are you going to cry, or keep it moving? Your mind, body and soul need you to keep it moving and handle the situation and move forward. What is your mindset? We all deal differently. Some of us never live up to what we set out to do because we never bounce back from some traumatic experiences. We must start reaching out to our world with confidence and rational thinking. We must get through it. Things are never as bad as they seem.

Reflection: Take away this fact that you are in control of you! How are you leading yourself?

What do you want from a leader? Why don't you give those things to you. You are able and capable. Get to it. We have a world to live in. We have life to speak and live. We have people that are watching us. Let's get to moving like we own ourselves.

Call to Action: How do we move like we own ourselves? First, we must tell ourselves this. It's not our jobs that dictate how we eat. It's our willingness to go work that job to get food on our table that dictates how we eat. There are a million things to do in this world, you picked your devotion. Find out what it is about that one thing in life that is "holding you back". I guarantee the common denominator will be YOU! Understand EVERYONE goes through hardships. One thing you can guarantee about life, is you will be hit. You will be hit hard! Guaranteed! We have the control of how hard that hit is. We can have a perspective of giving up after you are hit, or you can give a hit back! Be conscious of your reaction to things. You can really damage your momentum and dig a hole for yourself that you bury yourself in. Make it last for you!

# Conclusion

So, at the time of this writing, I am preparing myself to turn 40 in a few months. It is an exciting time for me. I am ready to embrace this journey. I have been asking several older people about what the 40s are like for them. I was talking to my "uncle" Tracy one day and he said, " man, youngblood, your 40's are when you conquer your world. You are the strongest physically, you know a little more about life and you aren't scared to execute." That hit me like a ton of bricks. As I said earlier, life is a bunch of chapters. Every chapter has a meaningful purpose and it adds to your overall "book".

What is your fight? What is your purpose? Who do you have around you? What do you want to accomplish? Are you bored? Do you think you have another life after this? What are you waiting for? These are questions that I've asked myself, and they were tough to answer. Some of these questions produce scary moments. Like, do you believe this is it, or you have your next lifetime to experience everything you ever wanted? Some of us walk through this life in pure routine. We let the wind blow us either way. Whatever the world allows us to do, we do. Whatever the laws of the land are, we follow. We follow blind leaders, even if we didn't elect them. We "go with the flow". You are going to need yourself to be more intentional with your moves. I'm not saying just go out and break the laws, and go nuts, but I am saying get to your life. Draw up your own desires and needs and execute. Map out a plan to live the life you want. If you want to travel more, set up a plan to make money as you travel, so you can keep ways to get paid. If you want to be healthier, create your own garden and grow your own foods. If you want to help people, you don't need a degree, just start helping people. If you want to earn more money, produce a product to sell for more than what it cost to make. You have the ability to build or destroy whatever you want. Love living and live to love.

Reflection: Too many times, we plan to fail by not planning. Planning is crucial. "Well sometimes planning doesn't work" is what I hear some of you saying. You are 100% right. Because for some reason, we put limits on our planning. We plan things out as far as we see the outcome. We don't plan to conquer various outcomes. Contingency plans should be at least 7 plays deep.

We understand the next chapter is ours, correct? Because the last chapter, you might agree that you didn't understand it was yours because of some of the choices you made. You can look back and see some of the "go with the flow" actions you had. Going forward, let's realize that our life is way more controllable than we allow. Maybe we need to learn to trust our own judgement.

Call to Action: Stop right now and live in the moment! You need to recognize what you are doing! Stop and ask yourself are you in control. What's your next moment going to look like? What are you doing to make it how you want it? What do you want? Every second is time ticking away. It is YOUR time ticking away. Every moment is yours. The more you practice controlling your thoughts GOING IN to your moments, the more you will see and understand it's on you. It's on you to make IT work. What is your IT?

I don't have all of the answers. But I feel a strong need to converse. I think conversations are important. Conversations are a launch pad to endless opportunity and life. What we say, think, and how we receive information is our foundation and how we navigate through the world. I remember some conversations I've had with individuals that literally happened decades ago. They are powerful conversations. Those conversations turned into reflections and more conversations with me. These moments guide and shape us. Who's team are you on? Yours? Well tell yourself this. Tell yourself this a lot. We need to hear it over and over. Just like when you were a kid and your mother had to tell you over and over to clean your room. After a while, having a clean room was important to you, but you had to be trained and told several times before it sank in.

Some of us will say we don't care how other's feel about us, but many of us actually do care. It is human to want to be liked. We like being invited to social gatherings, even if we decline the invite. But we must understand no one is obligated to like us. People dislike others for various reasons, beyond our control. The sooner in life you can accept this, the better. You won't need validation from others as often. You will understand that most people do not care about you. Don't take that personal! You came into this world by yourself, you will leave by yourself. Control yourself while you are here. Control your attitude.

Attitude! I am not going to act like I walk around like it's peaches and cream. It's not! Sometimes I struggle. But the attitude you bring into the world is a reflection of you. I constantly must check myself and make sure I find something positive in the current moment. I struggle like others with this. Sometimes a memory of my past may trip me into a sad and dark moment, but I constantly encourage myself to find something to smile about. Trust me, regardless how life is at the moment, there is ALWAYS something to smile about. The life is made up of constant disappointing times for us all. We don't have to dwell there. We don't have to stay in the dark. We consciously can snap our fingers and redirect our thinking. It sounds easy, well it is, once you have the desire and practice. What types of food am I consuming? This is probably one of the most important questions you need to ask yourself. Why? Because the food we eat determines the quality of our lives to some degree. Of course, we understand eating too many fried foods can lead to hypertension, high blood pressure, obesity, etc. We also understand that too much sugar and salt can have adverse effects on our bodies. But do you understand the foods we eat can make us sluggish mentally as well? Our diet is an extreme determining factor of what kind of attitude we will have. Pay close attention to your food consumption. There are so many reasons the foods we eat need to be healthy for your mind, body and soul. One obvious reason is that you want to live a long life, right? Well you definitely want to live a long and HEALTHY life. Your quality of life is just as important as the length of your life. If you aren't able to enjoy your life to the fullest because of constant pain and suffering, you don't want to wish this on anyone. Take care of your physical so you can have a healthy mentality. Learn how to eat to live, instead of live to eat.

The world needs you. The world needs your creativity, your opinion, and your good heart. The world needs your perspectives and examples for future leaders. Yes, you are an example. I don't care how unnoticed you think you are, someone is watching you. Someone is learning from you. People pay attention to everything. Some of us don't even realize we are paying attention until we are actually being led. You might be in front of that line people are following. Be conscious of this. Live every day knowing you are giving back to this world. What is it that I am giving back? Is it an incredible smile and positive attitude? Is it negative, toxic behavior? What can I add to this world? How can I change my surroundings? The food I consume bleeds out from the inside and reflects on my outside. So does the music I inject into my brain. The movies I watch, the books I read. Everything is a part of your arsenal. Imagine a police officer. What do you see? In order for him to do his job, he has to strap on a heavy utility belt full of tools that will aid and assist him. Ask yourself "what is in my belt that is helping/hurting me." What you have in your belt effects every aspect of your life. That police officer has to learn how to walk and sit comfortably with guns and night sticks and other tools. What tools are you bringing along on your walk? Build your life from the inside out. Work on you. Work on identifying things that you don't need in your belt. A lot of the stuff you may find just weighs you down. You may realize you are missing something that is vital. We all must self-evaluate often. Take a step back and adjust yourself. Be present and productive during this time so you can live your best life. I leave with saying, you are your own worst enemy because you are the only one that can impact your life negatively. No one can stop a determined, positive, conscious, and strong mind. Build.

www.ingramcontent.com/pod-product-compliance
Ingram Content Group UK Ltd.
Pitfield, Milton Keynes, MK11 3LW, UK
UKHW020414250726
13967UKWH00007B/2643
9 781716 739460